# English
## in the School Grounds

# *English*
## *in the School Grounds*

**Learning through Landscapes**

—— BRIAN KEANEY ——

**Learning through LANDSCAPES**

The Learning Through Landscapes Trust aims to heighten the awareness of Local Education Authority officers, school governors, parents, heads and teachers in schools, of the teaching and learning potential which exists in the school landscape. It seeks to stimulate changes in the quality and use of the land surrounding schools, to encourage the better use of existing resources for learning and to improve the environment within which learning takes place.

For further details, please contact:

The Information and Publicity Officer
Learning through Landscapes Trust
Third Floor
Southside Offices
The Law Courts
Winchester
Hants
SO23 9DL

Tel: (0962) 846258

SOUTHGATE

**First published 1993 by Southgate Publishers Ltd**

**Southgate Publishers Ltd**
**Glebe House, Church Street, Crediton,**
**Devon EX17 2AF**

Printed and bound in Great Britain by Short Run Press Ltd, Exeter, Devon.

**This book is printed on recycled paper.** The cover is printed on 240 gram Reprise Matt Board, the colour section on 115 gram Reprise Satin, and the main text on 90 gram Reprise Matt.

British Library Cataloguing in Publication Data.
A CIP catalogue record for this book is available from the British Library.

ISBN 1–85741–031–9

**ACKNOWLEDGEMENTS**
Poems are reprinted by permission of the following:

'Conkers' by Roland Nicholas by permission of The National Exhibition of Children's Art.
'Senses' by Ruth Kingshott, first published in *Young Words*, by permission of W H Smith. The poem was an award-winning entry in the 1986 W H Smith Young Writers' Competition.
'Water' by Charles Thomson by permission of the World Wide Fund for Nature.
'Storm' by permission of Nick Bartlett.
'Matilda' from Hilaire Belloc's *Cautionary Tales for Children* by permission of the Peters Fraser & Dunlop Group Ltd.

Photographs are reproduced by permission of the following:
colour section, p.3: 'Dig Where You Stand'/Living Archive Project 1990
colour section, p.4: (top) Learning through Landscapes/Andrew Jeffrey; (bottom) Learning through Landscapes/Bill Lucas
p.10 Clare Eastland
p.19 Poems on the Underground
p.26 Express & Echo Publications Ltd
pp.14, 25, 32 Learning through Landscapes/Susan Humphries
p.36 Learning through Landscapes
Other photographs were taken at St Michael's Combined School, Exeter.
The cover photograph was taken at Pilgrim Primary School, Plymouth.

# Contents

# Introduction

Anyone who has ever tried to sit down in front of a blank sheet of paper and write knows that this is not the most fruitful way of encouraging creativity. The best writing is born out of observation and experience. Surprisingly this well-known truth is not always acted upon in schools. Field trips, which are commonplace in other subjects, are relatively unknown in English.

The premise of this book, however, is that the school grounds provide a largely unexploited opportunity for just such field trips. They are a territory where the imagination can engage with reality; they exist within the management of the school authorities but seldom within their complete control.

For the grounds of the school are its wildlife park, where insects and animals carry on their discreet negotiations with humanity. It is in the school grounds that the seasons leave their unmistakable signature and it is here too that children create their most uninhibited dramas.

This book attempts to explore some of these possibilities by using school grounds as an inspiration for a series of activities in storytelling, poetry writing, drama and language work.

Each of the four main chapters takes as its point of departure a quotation from the National Curriculum document 'English for ages 5 to 16'. The activities which follow fulfil specific requirements for Attainment Targets in all three profile components of English: Speaking and Listening, Reading, and Writing.

The ideas in this book can be used by teachers of English even if their schools have only the most limited school grounds provision. Clearly, however, there is much to be gained from an imaginative development of the environment in which our children spend so much of their growing and learning time. The Learning Through Landscapes Trust was set up with the express purpose of encouraging the use of the school grounds as an educational resource and it is with the very clear intention of encouraging such development that this book has been written.

Much English teaching at Key Stages 1 and 2 is, of course, thematic in nature and taught in an integrated fashion. The activities described in this book are all presented in ways which readily fit into this approach and in many cases cross-refer to other subjects.

At the back of the book there is a small section of photocopiable (pupil) worksheets. One page gives information for teachers (or other adult helpers). The facing page can be photocopied for pupils' use.

Many of the ideas suggested in these pages are eminently down to earth. Others may take pupils by surprise but, as Jill Pirrie has observed in *On Common Ground*, 'Our children must learn that if their poetry is to work it must surprise'.

To get the best out of our children we need constantly to present them with new challenges. Teachers will certainly find in this book an approach to the subject that is fresh and effective. It is hoped that in doing so they will find an opportunity to increase their pleasure in teaching English.

The school grounds can provide inspiration for a wide range of English activities. While stories acquire special charm when read outside, creative language work arises out of first-hand observation.

# Story

The story is one of the most fundamental methods of human communication. When a child tells the teacher 'I fell and cut my knee' he or she is telling a story – a short one certainly, but one to which the storyteller would no doubt be prepared to add detail and colour, given any encouragement.

Children instinctively tell stories, arranging the world into heroes and villains. Often they need the help of adults to sort out the real from the imagined. However, it is essential that in doing so teachers or parents do not stifle a child's imagination. We run the risk of doing this when we limit the scope of storytelling.

One way in which the potential for storytelling is sometimes limited is the tendency for processes, which start as ways of accessing the imagination, to become rigid and so lose their potency. If stories are always received from teachers or from books, or written on paper, at a table in the classroom, for example, there is a risk that the whole thing can become stale and predictable.

Teachers are aware of this and seek ways to stimulate children's own creativity. Placing the story outside, in a tangible location, is one way of encouraging this process and it can have a liberating effect on the child's imagination.

## Minibeast stories

Minibeast stories are popular with children. Try reading some well-known insect tales first, such as *The Very Hungry Caterpillar* or *The Very Cross Ladybird* by Erich Carle. Ask the children what other minibeasts they know.

Now take the children out into the school grounds. Ask each child to find four things:

- a minibeast;
- something else that is alive or was alive (e.g. a leaf);
- something that was never alive (e.g. a stone);
- something with water in it.

You may need to talk to them first about which things are alive, which were once alive, and which have never been alive.

You might also like to add a fifth object, one which they can chose for themselves. Tell the children that the objects can be either big or small. For instance, the object with water in it could be a bottle-top or it might be a pond.

You will probably not want the children to pick the objects up, or bring them back to the classroom, but you will need to make a list, as you go along, of everything they discover. When you return to the classroom the children can each draw the objects they have found and write out their names. Depending on the developmental stage of the children, these lists may be words, approximations to words or just letters.

Now make up a story about a minibeast, involving the things the class has found. Afterwards ask the children to make up their own minibeast stories.

The children might like to develop other stories about the minibeasts that live in the school. They could try to imagine their lives. Ask questions like:

- What does the minibeast eat?
- Are the children cruel or kind to the minibeast?
- Are they frightened of it?
- What does it think of them?
- Who are its enemies?
- How does the weather affect it?

## On this spot

AT1iii–v
AT3iii–v

A sense of place is an important part of story-telling. Books for younger children often supply this in the illustrative detail. Older children enjoy stories like *The Hobbit* or the *Narnia* stories, which are based upon power-fully realized imaginary worlds. Unfortunately, most of us tend to shut out the world that surrounds us. This is particularly true of the workplace or, for children, the school.

'On This Spot' is a game which encourages spontaneous storytelling as well as focusing attention on the immediate environment. Children are asked to make up stories about extraordinary events that might have happened on a particular spot in the school grounds.

It is worthwhile dwelling on the idea that a place can have its own history. If there are any plaques near your school commemorating the spot where some famous person lived or where some historical event took place, it may be worth taking the children to see it and doing some research into the person or the event recorded.

Take them on a walk around the school grounds. What is the oldest thing that they can find? Are there any clues in the building about the way life was lived in the past? There may be bootscrapers, for example, or separate entrances for girls and boys. Are there trees and hedges on the site? If so, how old are they?

You could also talk to them about what might have been on the site before the school was built. How much local history can they find out?

One source of local history could be the reminiscences of an older person – perhaps a

A plaque recording the home of a famous person can provide a focus for research into the school's locality.

grandparent or a former member of the staff. This person could be invited into the school to talk about the area as it was in the past. Before the visit, the children can think of questions to ask.

When they have gathered all the information the children could make a time line, linking local and world events, such as the Second World War, the first landing on the moon, class 4B starting school and so on.

What about pre-historic events? You might like to read a time-slip story (i.e. a story in which the characters are transported to another period in time) with the children, such as *Moondial* by Helen Cresswell.

They could chose their own places to focus on or you might find it easier to mark certain spots with chalk in advance and ask the children to find them.

The stories which the children create can be quite short and need not all be entirely serious. They may also serve as starting points for longer, perhaps written, narratives.

T1i–v
T3i–v

## *Last night in the playground...*

The school grounds can be used as a starting point for innumerable stories. 'Last Night in the Playground' is another game which uses a formula to generate narrative.

Divide the children into groups and ask them to go into different areas and make up a story about something that happened last night in the playground. Give each group the beginning of the story. For younger children the words 'Last night in the playground I ...' will probably be enough. Older or more able children might be able to extend their ideas into small narratives. The following is a list of suggestions that they might enjoy exploring, but teachers may prefer to develop their own.

### Story starting points

Last night in the playground I ...

   ... saw a ghost.

   ... heard the sound of someone digging.

   ... saw a strange machine.

   ... heard a sound like a wild animal.

   ... smelled burning.

   ... heard someone shouting for help.

**Last night in the playground ... the strangest things happened!**

Each group member must add to the story. To help them build up the story you could ask questions like the following.

- What were they doing there?
- How did they get in?
- How did they feel when they saw the ghost or the strange machine?
- Were they seen by anyone?

## *Chinese whispers*

AT1i–iii

As well as being spontaneous, storytelling can also be a remembered activity. This is the way stories were passed down before writing. You could discuss this with the children. Ask them if anyone has ever told them – rather than read them – a story: a parent or grandparent, for example. Talk about the process of exaggeration. Ask them whether people always tell the truth or whether they sometimes exaggerate. Do stories ever change when they are passed on from one person to another? Ask them to imagine how stories would change if they were passed between hundreds of different people.

A game that children can play in the school grounds, and which illustrates this concept, is 'Chinese Whispers'. The children sit in a circle and pass a sentence round by whispering it from one to another. By the time the message has returned to its source it has very often changed beyond recognition.

This is one occasion when external acoustics are a distinct advantage. In a classroom there is a danger that the message might be overheard. The outdoor environment – with wind, traffic noise, birdsong, etc. – tends to prevent this.

As with all activities, it helps if you can find a nice spot in the school grounds to carry it out. If you are lucky enough to have trees on your site, you could sit the children in a circle round a big tree. This helps to create a sense of distance over which the message must travel. It is a good idea also to prepare the messages in advance and write them on pieces of paper to hand to the first child.

You might like to utilize fully the space that school grounds provide by extending a game of 'Chinese Whispers' over a large area. Instead of having the children sitting in a circle, ask them to stand at a considerable distance from each other. Each child must then walk up to the next to pass on the message, and then take up the position vacated by the next player, who moves on in turn.

AT1i–viii
AT3i–viii

## A story bazaar

One way of recreating the spread of stories from one community to another is to set up a story chain. This can be done from class to class within a school or even between schools. The idea is to pass on a story from one group to another in a circle of communication so that it returns to the original tellers. This is not as formidable a task as it sounds.

You will need to decide what sort of material to use. The simplest chain involves children receiving stories from their teachers. Clearly there can be a lack of ownership about this and some teachers prefer to work with children over a period of time to develop the children's own stories. It might be helpful to adopt a theme for the chain: animal stories, for example, or stories from different cultures.

How you organize your telling will depend to a very considerable extent on your own experience with the class. Stories can be narrated by individuals in sequence; there can be one narrator, perhaps the teacher, with others taking character parts; the story could be dramatized, with a chorus narrating the action. Because of the size of most classes, it is likely that you will want to divide the class into groups. The different groups can work on parts of the same story, or on separate stories.

A story chain can be conducted indoors but by placing it outdoors, as part of a story bazaar, it can be given wider uses. The whole school could now be involved, perhaps as part of a Bookweek.

This can be as lively a spectacle as you choose to make it. The grounds can be decorated with flags and bunting. Other classes from the school, parents and teachers can all form the audience. The children telling stories can make their own costumes. Other children, particularly the younger ones, will enjoy dressing up as characters from well-known books or fairy tales. A local bookshop might be interested in putting on a display. Your school might like to invite a professional storyteller or an author to come along to add to the sense of occasion.

The children who have participated in the story chain could set up storytelling stalls. These could be like market stalls, using trestle tables, with posters, perhaps showing scenes from the story. Props used in the storytelling could be set out on the tables. Alternatively the 'stalls' could be small areas roped off and enclosed by rounders bases or chairs, marked out with chalk.

The children could develop their own street cries, like market traders, to call the audience to hear them perform their stories.

Children can set up their own storytelling stalls.

The story telling is best organized as a promenade performance (see page 32). This allows the audience to walk around the stalls and hear the different stories. Stories can follow each other in sequence or more than one storytelling can take place simultaneously, allowing different sections of the audience to hear different stories at the same time.

Simultaneous storytelling gives more of the feel of a market or bazaar and a school's grounds are usually large enough to prevent one performance from drowning out another.

This method also has the advantage of taking some of the pressure off the children, who are not placed so much in the spotlight if there are other performances taking place at the same time. Of course, they may need to repeat their performance so that each section of the audience hears it. It is a good idea, therefore, to organize pre-arranged times for groups to tell their stories.

## Story trails

So far we have dealt almost exclusively with oral storytelling. But reading or being read to is also an activity which can very readily be transferred to the school grounds. Any story is given a new charm when children hear it out of doors. But rather than just employing this as an occasional device for a hot day, why not make it a sustained project taking place over a period of days or weeks?

### 1. A LISTENING TRAIL

Stories can be given a special atmosphere by reading them outside. Look for stories which link with locations in your school grounds. A story like the 'Three Pigs', for example, might be dramatized by using play structures or other features of the grounds which the children could imagine were the pigs' houses.

What you have made in this way is a story trail. It can be used over and over again. Your school might like to reinforce the trail by painting symbols on the ground in the same way that some schools have identified nature walks by a line of green footprints or some other emblematic device. How about a series of opened books painted on the ground? Alternatively the children could create their own guide books to the story trail for visitors or younger children (see page 40). Each story should be read at a different location and you might like to ask the children to make a map, or a series of pictures, showing where each reading took place. The children could also find stories of their own to read aloud and suggest locations for them.

Some time after the reading, it is a useful follow-up device to take the children back to the same location in which they heard a story to talk about it and to tell it in their own words. Ask questions like: What did you like or dislike about the story? How much of it do you remember? What helped you to remember?

**Storytelling in different locations can be linked into a listening trail.**

## 2. A MYTHICAL TRAIL

A story trail is simply a device for focusing imagination, a concrete form of the mnemonic. It helps to dramatize stories in the minds of children. Myths and legends are often particularly suitable for exploring in this way and using a story trail can help to make them more resonant in children's minds.

Many myths are essentially peripatetic. For example, the story of the wandering of Odysseus after the Trojan war, his different adventures with the Cyclops, with Circe, with the Lotos Eaters, among others, all happened in different places. Why not explore each story in a different location in the school?

Features of individual myths can be dramatized. One example is the story of Theseus who found his way out of the labyrinth by unrolling a ball of string. This can be literally dramatized, whether or not you are able to create a maze in your school grounds.

You should read or tell the children the story of Theseus and the Labyrinth first. There are a number of versions available. The basic story is given opposite.

When the children are familiar with the plot, talk about the details of the story. What must it have been like in the dark underground labyrinth?

Divide the children into pairs and give each pair a ball of string. Tell one child to hold the end of the ball of string while the other makes a journey, unrolling the string as he or she goes. When the ball of string is exhausted, ask the first child to retrace the journey with eyes closed.

Not only do story trails create a sense of occasion about reading stories, they also serve as a real, physical manifestation of the structure that underlies connected narrative. When children first begin writing narrative for themselves they are reluctant to get involvedin the sort of planning that is necessary to string together anything but the most simple series of events. Nevertheless, through watching television and reading books, they often have high expectations of stories and want to produce highly complex plots themselves. A story trail can assist them in this process.

Older children will enjoy revisiting the mythical trail and creating their own mythical character, who encounters a series of adventures.

**At Coombes School a turf maze has been created.**

# Theseus and the Labyrinth

Long ago, Minos was king of the Greek island of Crete. He was a fierce king and a fearless warrior. One day he was brought the news that his son had been killed in Athens. Minos had loved his son dearly and he sought a terrible revenge on the people of Athens. He conquered their city and threatened to destroy it totally, killing every man and woman in it.

The people of Athens begged him for mercy. Minos agreed to spare them but only on condition that each year they sent to Crete seven young men and seven young women. These were to sail to the island in a ship with black sails, like a funeral ship, for they would never return. Minos would feed them to a terrible monster called the Minotaur, which he kept locked in an underground maze, known as the Labyrinth. The Minotaur was half bull and half man and it lived on human flesh.

The Athenians agreed: they had no choice. Year after year the sacrifice continued until one day Theseus, the son of the Athenian king, decided he would go as one of the young people to be sacrificed. His father tried to stop him but he was determined. He said that he would kill the monster and return in the boat and he would change its sails to white.

Minos, king of Crete, laughed bitterly when he heard that Theseus was among the party of Athenians. Now the king of Athens would know what it was like to lose a son, he thought to himself. But his daughter, Ariadne, was impressed with Theseus. He had been brave enough to risk his life. She decided to help him. She knew that killing the Minotaur was only half the problem. If he succeeded in this, he still had to find his way out of the Labyrinth and no one knew its secret.

When Theseus was being taken to the entrance to the Labyrinth she gave him a ball of thread which she told him to use to find his way out.

Theseus wandered through the maze until he found the monster and, after a difficult fight, slew it. Then he rewound the ball of string and escaped with his comrades. That night they boarded ship and set off for home.

Sadly, in his excitement, Theseus did not remember to change the ship's sails to white ones. When the ship drew near to Athens the king, his father, saw the black sails and assumed that Theseus had failed. Before the boat had put into harbour, the old king had died of grief.

# Poetry

*Children in primary-school playgrounds clearly demonstrate an instinctive pleasure in rhythm, pattern and rhyme. But this will need constant nurturing if it is to develop into an appreciation of the richness of poetry, where words are 'alive with a plurality of meanings from their contexts, their associations and their sensory qualities'. (7.1)*

When you consider what poetry actually is, it seems extraordinary that children are so seldom allowed to study it out of doors. It is an example of the requirements of the subject being subordinated to the demands of day-to-day organization.

Poetry is a delicate thing, difficult to define or even explain, but clearly it abounds with descriptions of places and things in terms of their interaction with the human psyche. It is a mixture of atmosphere and mood, observation and analysis. All this can be achieved within the confines of four walls, of course. But how strange it is to see children reading poems about trees, about the wind, about birds, puddles, rainbows, shadows, or whatever, always separated from the subject by sheets of glass.

To enjoy poetry it may only be necessary to hear its music, as babies and young children listen to nursery rhymes. But to understand poetry it is necessary to observe. Teaching poetry then begins with teaching children to look.

## Above and below

AT1i–v
AT3i–v

Take the children into the school grounds. Ask them to notice everything above the level of their heads. At first they may see nothing remarkable, only the sky and rooftops. Ask them to look for detail: cloud formations, the colours of roof-tiles, birds in flight, aeroplane trails, and so on.

Then tell the children to look down and to notice everything they see at ground level: cracks in the tarmac, insects scurrying about, leaves lying on the ground. Now take them to another spot, with a different perspective. What difference does this make to their observations?

Ask the children to make lists of what they have observed. Many poets, from Shakespeare to Walt Whitman, have used lists and listing as a powerful poetic device.

**Encourage children to notice detail when they look up.**

AT1i–v
AT3i–v

AT3i–v

## Sensory walks

Another way of showing children how to tune into their senses is to take them for a sensory walk.

Take them for a walk around the grounds. Ask them to concentrate on the senses. What can they hear? It helps if they shut their eyes. At first all the sounds will seem merged into one, but gradually they will begin to distinguish the individual notes in the whole sound picture.

What can they feel? Wind? Sunshine? What can they smell? Ask them to touch the walls of the school, the bark of trees.

Now ask them to look around. How do objects look in relationship to each other: the school against the sky, the fence against grass, for example? What details can they see in the buildings? Are they old, crumbling, peeling, smart, modern, damp? Ask them to bring back something from their walk – perhaps a stone, a twig or a leaf – to help remind them of the feelings they discovered.

When you return from your walk, ask the children to find words to describe the experience. You might find it helpful to give them some to begin with. Ask them to concentrate on finding very specific words to describe how things smelled or felt. Make lists of the words on large sheets of paper and display them in the classroom.

When the children have been introduced to this notion of creative observation and have practised it several times, they are ready to begin structuring their experiences into poems.

**By covering their eyes children will concentrate on their other senses.**

## The Five Senses

Too much emphasis on structure can sometimes be inhibiting but at other times it can provide a source of poetic inspiration in itself.

One way of providing this kind of aid to inspiration is to reconstruct the process of sensuous experience from memory, dwelling with the same luxuriant attention on the language and expression used, as in this example, written by a school pupil.

---

### Senses

Taste
The dry, musty leaves
Which tamper with the air.
Lingering smoke,
The taste of ash.

Hear
The clip of the shears
As they prune the hedge.
Listen to the leaves
As they throw a tantrum
In the wind.

Smell
The sweet fragrance
From soft brown apples
Feasted by wasps,
The dusty corn
Thrown from the yellow harvester.

See
The rust colour
Painted through the garden.
See the bee,
Flying,
Weighed down by boots of yellow pollen.

Touch
The leaves
Crumbling with dryness.
Feel the bitter night
In the air
Of my autumn garden.

**Ruth Kingshott**

---

## *Focusing down*

The way in which an environment expands as you get closer to it can be explored in the school grounds by focusing on detail. Ask the children to bring back objects from plants or trees, such as conkers, pieces of bark, leaves, twigs or seeds. You may want them to choose parts of the plants that have already fallen or broken off.

They can bring them back to the classroom and draw them. They might like to use magnifying glasses to look at the objects in greater detail.

Ask the children also to think about what the objects remind them of. Comparisons may be quite fanciful. They should feel free to pursue them, however unlikely, since the purpose is to see the object in a different light.

## *Naming of places*

One very important aspect of the school grounds is its atmosphere. This is something we try to influence in a number of ways, by planting trees, creating seating areas or putting in playground markings, for example. But we often neglect the naming process.

Giving an area a name creates a sense of identification with it. It is also a way for the children to express their feelings about the school grounds in language.

Begin by doing some preliminary work on place names. Where does the school name come from? What are your local borough, village or parish names?

### Conkers

Like lots of small
Light green hedgehogs,
With sharp spikes
On their backs,
Lying on the grass.
Inside are chocolate brown conkers,
Smooth, round and cold.

**Roland Nicholas (age 8)**

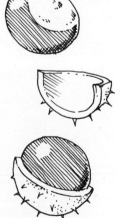

Back in the classroom, objects found outside can be drawn and described.

The poet Walter de la Mare says of English place names, 'They have a meaning well worth the discovering, but meanwhile they are curious, romantic, echoing sounds merely to hear and utter.' He goes on to cite lists of extraordinary and evocative names of towns, villages, woods and fields. The following is only a smattering:

> Columbine, the Culvery, Spanyard,
> Cold Blow, Knockjohn, Homer Corner,
> Oase Edge, Lunie Park, Flints, Lily Field,
> Monticroft, Hatchetty, Parliament Close,
> Allhollows, Mammonds.

If possible, take the children on a walk to observe the local street names. If not, study a map. How do councils choose names when new roads are built?

Now ask the children to think of their own names for areas in the school. So often this is something that is neglected when other aspects of a school are considered. Teachers talk of 'the upper playground' or 'the grassed area', for example. The children could make maps of the school, showing the areas they have named. They could also make their own signposts.

Once a place has a name it can be the focus for a poem. Many ancient peoples believed that each place had its own presiding spirit or genius, which protected that area and dwelt in it unseen. The character of such a spirit was defined by the place where it dwelt. Ask the children to imagine the spirit of one of the places they have named. What would it be like – friendly or unfriendly? What would it see when it looked out? How would it feel about the way people treated the place where it lived? If it could speak, what would it say?

## Poetry murals

Another way of giving a distinctive atmosphere to specific areas in your school grounds, and at the same time associating poetry with place in the minds of children, is to set up poetry murals. This is an idea made use of by the London Underground, when in 1986 it began putting up poems in the advertising spaces in tube trains.

Poetry murals can be made very easily by typing or writing poems on card and laminating them. These can then have a hole punched in them, for threading string through. They can be hung up in different parts of the grounds.

Of course bigger murals could be painted on to hardboard. This is something which you might like the children to do themselves.

The effect of these murals is to create a gradual, almost subliminal exposure to verse, in which poetry becomes a part of the landscape. However they do need to be changed regularly, perhaps every half term. Otherwise, as with any display, children, and adults too, cease to notice them.

Children could also produce their own poetry murals. They could do this by choosing poems they like from anthologies or ones that they have written themselves.

## A poetry treasure hunt

A poetry treasure hunt is a way of using the physical space of the school grounds to explore meaning in poetry. Begin by making cards with poems written on them, rather like

'Will you walk a little faster?' said a whiting to a snail,
'There's a porpoise close behind us, and he's treading on my tail.
See how eagerly the lobsters and the turtles all advance!
They are waiting on the shingle – will you come and join the dance?
*Will you, won't you, will you, won't you, will you join the dance? Will you, won't you, will you, won't you, won't you join the dance?*
'You can really have no notion how delightful it will be
When they take us up and throw us, with the lobsters, out to sea!'
But the snail replied 'Too far, too far!', and gave a look askance –
Said he thanked the whiting kindly, but he would not join the dance.
*Would not, could not, would not, could not, would not join the dance. Would not, could not, would not, could not, could not join the dance.*
'What matters it how far we go?' his scaly friend replied.
'There is another shore, you know, upon the other side.
The further off from England the nearer is to France –
Then turn not pale, beloved snail, but come and join the dance.
*Will you, won't you, will you, won't you, will you join the dance? Will you, won't you, will you, won't you, won't you join the dance?*'

**THE**

**LOBSTER**

**QUADRILLE**

Lewis Carroll
(1832–1898)

⊖ **Poems on the Underground**
The British Council · The British Library (Stefan Zweig Programme) · Copies of this poster may be
obtained from London Transport Museum Shop, Covent Garden, FREEPOST, London WC2E 7BR.

**Poems turn up in unlikely places! This is one of a series of posters placed in London Underground trains.**

A poetry treasure hunt: when the children have found all the lines they can try to reassemble the poems.

your poetry murals, and cutting them up into individual lines or small groups of lines.

The poems can then be placed in different spots around the school grounds and clues given as to their whereabouts, or perhaps a map made. Alternatively, if your playground has a grid, you could place the lines on different squares and ask the children to use co-ordinates to find them.

Children can then begin the hunt. When they have collected all the lines, they can try to reassemble the poems. For younger children you can use well-known poems or nursery rhymes. For older children you may wish to choose more difficult poetry.

When they have reassembled the poems, ask the children to say what they think each poem means. Often children will reassemble poems according to a sense of mood rather than because of logical clues. This itself is a useful starting point for further work on writing poetry.

## Poetry jigsaws

AT2i-

A variation on a treasure hunt using entire poems is one which uses only snatches of poetry. At the end of the hunt the children will have found half a dozen or so individual lines. These can be lines from different poems or lines from the same poem.

Very young children can use lines from nursery rhymes, such as:

All the king's horses and all the king's men
The maid was in the garden, hanging out the clothes
The little dog laughed to see such fun

Now you can ask them if they can remember the rest of the rhymes, or what other stories could be made out of these lines.

Older children can use lines such as:

When I opened my eyes this morning
This is the key of the kingdom

'Is there anybody there ?' said the Traveller

They might like to use each line as the starting point for a poem of their own or try to fit them all into one poem or story.

## Inscriptions

Also worth looking at with children are verse inscriptions. A visit to a nearby graveyard to look for epitaphs can be very interesting. Mottoes or inscriptions of other kinds are often found on public buildings such as libraries, monuments and sometimes on schools.

Why not hold a competition to devise the best inscription to put over a school entrance or archway?

## Elemental poetry

Few people can agree on a definition of what exactly poetry is. Perhaps this is because in poetry there exists a sort of crack in the control we exercise over the environment through language. Poetry allows the wildness of nature a way back into our domestic world. Children instinctively understand this. In the same way that their behaviour becomes scattier and less controllable on windy days, so too can they be induced to write wonderful poetry by focusing on the elemental processes of nature.

It is all very well doing this from inside a classroom, but there is nothing like taking the children outside when the wind is blustering, or after a rainstorm to look at the freshly minted puddles.

Why not also hold readings of elemental poetry outside? So much poetry sounds really splendid when read aloud outside. Choose poems that focus on the forces of nature, like those reproduced here. Get the children to rehearse reading them aloud. You might also like to add other symbolic elements to your reading, making up your own ceremonies.

**Feeling the wind can lead to some powerful elemental poetry.**

## Water

Water's found - as nature rules -
in many shapes: ponds, rivers, pools,
streams, lakes, drops, trickles, splashes,
showers,
canned, bottled, in the stems of flowers,

not to mention leaves, roots, petals,
also trees and often kettles,

tea pots, tea cups, fizzy drinks,
toilets, baths, bowls, buckets, sinks,

gurgling full of leaves down drains,
pouring in torrential rains,

pumped out by the heart in blood,
churned in earth to squelchy mud,

used by dad to wash his car,
mixed in jam inside a jar,

pounding round a washing machine,
keeping lawns a decent green,

squirting out of water pistols,
forming snow from tiny crystals,

making medicines and lotions,
filling earth with massive oceans.

There's something magical about it.
Where would we all be without it?

**Charles Thomson**

## The North Wind

The north wind doth blow,
And we shall have snow,
And what will poor robin do then,
poor thing?

He'll sit in a barn
And keep himself warm,
And hide his head under his wing,
poor thing.

**(Traditional)**

## Who Has Seen The Wind?

Who has seen the wind?
    Neither I nor you:
But when the leaves hang trembling
    The wind is passing thro'.

Who has seen the wind?
    Neither you nor I:
But when the trees bow down their heads
    The wind is passing by.

**Christina Rossetti**

## All in June

A week ago I had a fire,
  To warm my feet, my hands and face;
Cold winds, that never make a friend,
  Crept in and out of every place.

Today the fields are rich in grass,
  And buttercups in thousands grow;
I'll show the World where I have been -
  With gold-dust seen on either shoe.

Till to my garden back I come,
  Where bumble-bees, for hours and hours,
Sit on their soft, fat, velvet bums,
  To wriggle out of hollow flowers.

**W. H. Davies**

## Storm

Bursting on the suburbs with relentless gusts of energy
And concentrated fury comes the mad March gale
Blowing off the roofing felt which lies across the garden sheds
And patterning the window with a splash of sleet and hail.

Distending all the trousers on the wildly waving washing line;
Drumming on the window like a hanged man's heels
Swaying all the sculpture of the television aerials,
Muddying the roadway underneath the turning wheels.

Ear lobes reddening at the slashing of the hailstones,
Nose tips deadening at the coldness of the sleet,
Eyelids wincing at the brightness of the lightning,
Wet stones glistening beneath the hurried feet.

White marbles bouncing on the flat roofs of the garages,
Black sky paling as the storm dies down.
Wet folk emerging from the haven of a doorway
As the sun comes out again and smiles upon the town.

**Nick Bartlett**

## Here We Come A-Piping

Here we come a-piping,
In Springtime and in May
Green fruit a-ripening,
And Winter fled away.

The queen she sits upon the strand,
Fair as lily, white as wand;
Seven billows on the sea,
Horses riding fast and free,
And bells beyond the sand.

**Traditional**

## It is He

It is He who sends down
Rain from the sky,
From it ye drink,
And out of it grows
The vegetation on which
Ye feed your cattle.

With it He produces
For you corn, olives,
Date-palms, grapes,
And every kind of fruit:
Verily this is a Sign
For those who give thought.

**from the Qur'an**

# Matilda,
## Who told Lies, and was Burned to Death.

It happened that a few Weeks later
Her Aunt was off to the Theatre
To see that Interesting Play
*The Second Mrs. Tanqueray.*
She had refused to take her Niece
To hear this Entertaining Piece:
A Deprivation Just and Wise
To Punish her for Telling Lies.
That Night a Fire did break out –
You should have heard Matilda Shout!
You should have heard her Scream and Bawl,
And throw the window up and call
To People passing in the Street –
(The rapidly increasing Heat
Encouraging her to obtain
Their confidence) – but all in vain!
For every time She shouted 'Fire!'
They only answered 'Little Liar!'
And therefore when her Aunt returned,
Matilda, and the House, were Burned.

Matilda told such Dreadful Lies,
It made one Gasp and Stretch one's Eyes;
Her Aunt, who, from her Earliest Youth,
Had kept a Strict Regard for Truth,
Attempted to Believe Matilda:
The effort very nearly killed her,
And would have done so, had not She
Discovered this Infirmity.
For once, towards the Close of Day,
Matilda, growing tired of play,
And finding she was left alone,
Went tiptoe to the Telephone
And summoned the Immediate Aid
Of London's Noble Fire-Brigade.
Within an hour the Gallant Band
Were pouring in on every hand,
From Putney, Hackney Downs and Bow,
With Courage high and Hearts a-glow
They galloped, roaring through the Town,
'Matilda's House is Burning Down!'
Inspired by British Cheers and Loud
Proceeding from the Frenzied Crowd,
They ran their ladders through a score
Of windows on the Ball Room Floor;
And took Peculiar Pains to Souse
The Pictures up and down the House,
Until Matilda's Aunt succeeded
In showing them they were not needed
And even then she had to pay
To get the Men to go away!

**Burning a cardboard house: under controlled conditions children experience the element of fire.**

## Touched by fire

**T2i–viii**

The elements invariably leave their signatures on the landscape to touch our imaginations. Children are perhaps used to observing the rain fall, feeling the wind, playing on the muddy ground. Less commonly do they get a chance to observe fire.

Teachers are, understandably, wary of introducing fire into their lessons, but, under controlled conditions, it will exercise a powerful hold on children's imaginations. Nevertheless, teachers may need to show sensitivity in carrying out this activity and take into account the personalities of the children in their class.

Read Hilaire Belloc's cautionary tale 'Matilda', reproduced opposite, about a girl who plays with matches and eventually burns down her house.

Now invite the children to make their own house out of cardboard boxes, like the kind that supermarkets throw out. Allow them to give their house as much detail as possible, making a pitched roof, wallpapering the inside, drawing in details of furniture.

Ask them to bring old or broken objects which they no longer want, to put into the house: old socks, gloves, broken toys, postcards or diaries - anything that they themselves have used. Make sure each child has contributed something.

When the children have completed the house take it outside into the school grounds. Set it up in a space where it is well clear of anything that might catch alight. Keeping the children well back, set fire to the house.

After the burning, retrieve the contents, by sieving through the ash. Ask the children to try to identify anything of theirs.

This is an extremely powerful imaginative exercise. Now ask the children to write their own poem about a fire. They will undoubtedly have been affected by what they have witnessed and it will show in their writing.

## Walking the bounds

AT1i–viii

Elements of traditional customs or rituals can often be adapted and used as ceremonies for celebrating the school's environment and focusing language on the landscape and the elements. The practice of walking the bounds was once carried out annually throughout the country.

Traditionally parish or manorial boundaries were fixed by ceremonially walking them in procession once a year. At boundary markers, such as walls, milestones, streams or boulders, the procession would halt and recite a blessing or a passage from scripture. Sometimes boys were also thrown over boundary stones and beaten or tossed into clumps of nettles! Later this was replaced by a token bumping, not unlike 'the bumps' which traditionally accompany a child's birthday.

Walking the bounds of your school is an excellent way of extending the sense of ownership to children and teachers alike. Children might like to make their own costumes for this ceremony and perhaps carry sticks to beat the boundaries. Parents and school governors might also be invited. At regular intervals the procession could stop and stage a poetry reading.

A host of other traditional customs can be used in this manner. In many places wells or trees are decorated at specific times of the year. Bawming the Thorn, for example, is a ceremony originating near Warrington in Cheshire in which a hawthorn tree is decorated and danced round each year by the local children.

Many of these ceremonies already have their own accompanying verses, such as these lines, given new meaning by changing fashions, chanted on the last Thursday of October in Hinton St George, near Yeovil:

It's a Punky Night tonight
It's a Punky Night tonight
Give us a candle, give us a light
Adam and Eve wouldn't believe
It's a punky night tonight

Walking the bounds is still carried out in some parishes, giving children a direct link with the traditions of their ancestors.

# Drama

Drama is one of the key ways in which children can gain an understanding of themselves and of others, can gain confidence in themselves as decision-makers and problem-solvers, can learn to function collaboratively, and can explore - within a supportive framework - not only a range of human feelings, but also a whole spectrum of social situations and/or moral dilemmas. (8.6)

A lot of drama in schools takes place in environments that are far from ideal: in classrooms, for example, when the teacher is constantly aware that he or she might be disturbing the next class; or in the school hall while the dinner staff are preparing meals in the background.

The school grounds, however, offer possibilities that are frequently neglected. The children will already be using them for a variety of improvisational, movement, co-ordination and co-operation skills in the games they play in the playground.

Many of these are traditional and have been passed down over the generations by word of mouth. The open-ended structures of these games, however, usually allow them to assimilate contemporary material very quickly and many show interesting new twists. As our society becomes increasingly multi-cultural, new influences are being felt and children are playing games in the playground which originate from a diversity of cultures.

It is worth investigating these games, talking about them with the children, getting them to play them and to write out the rules. In this way you can compile your own school playground games book.

Begin by talking to the children about the games they are familiar with, and playing some well-known ones, such as 'Follow My Leader' or 'Simple Simon Says'.

Children employ skills of imagination and improvisation in the games they play outside.

**AT1i–iii**
**AT2i–viii**

## Minefield

The basic concept of 'Follow My Leader' can be extended into trust games. Much of drama is essentially collaborative. All of it depends on trust.

'Minefield' is a game which helps build up trust between partners and it is very simple to play. It involves two partners, one of whom is 'seeing' and one 'non-seeing'.

Begin by asking the children to imagine what it would be like not to be able to see. Take them for a walk in the school grounds and talk about what they can see. Now ask them to close their eyes and imagine that they only had their other senses to rely on. What would that be like?

Ask them to open their eyes again and to move away from each other, so that there is plenty of space between them. Now ask them to close their eyes and walk ten steps in any direction. When they have done that, ask them to describe how it felt.

Now tell them each to find a partner. Explain that one is to keep his or her eyes closed (or blindfolds could be used). The other will lead the first one around a series of obstacles.

You will need to decide how complex you want the obstacle course to be. You could simply take advantage of the existing features of the school grounds: for example, twice round the tree, along the nature path, and so on. Alternatively, you might like to try putting objects on the ground: chairs, boxes, books, rounders bases or simply chalk marks.

There are various ways in which the non-seeing child can be led. The seeing child can simply take his or her hand and this is definitely the best way to start. But you might like to advance to other methods, such as both children holding on to either end of a skipping rope.

Older children can be asked to negotiate the course without any touching. The non-seeing child should be led simply by instructions called by his or her partner.

When the children have played 'Minefield' ask them to sit down and produce a piece of creative writing from the point of view of someone with a visual disability. The response is always informed by the dramatic process they have been through.

---

In Great John's Hospital in the children's ward I lay with my eyes covered with bandages and the doctor on his way to take them off. I lay there with my parents at my side in silence, listening to the other children, shouting, screaming, laughing and playing with the nurses. At this time I was only 11 years old when I was in a car accident with my mum and dad. They only got a bruising and one or two cuts. But me, I came flying from the back seat of the car and through the front wind-screen and landed on the floor. This was all because the ball the boys were playing with went in the road and one of them ran out into the road without looking to get the ball. My dad slammed on the brakes and this is the result - me in hospital probably blind and that boy is still probably playing football and putting someone else in hospital.

The doctor had arrived with a nurse. I knew that because the doctor was talking to my parents while the nurse was drawing the curtain, pulling the blankets back and sitting me up. The doctor began to take the bandages off one side, then the other. He took the pads off my eyes. I opened them. I screamed. It was still dark. I could still not see anything. The doctor asked if I could see and I screamed louder, then shouted, 'No! No! I can't. I'm blind, aren't I? I'm blind. I'm blind.'

**Mark (11 years)**

---

## Walking into trouble

**AT1i–v**

This is a game to play once the children have been introduced to the notion of mime through games like 'Simple Simon Says'. It really allows the children to exploit the space that school grounds provide.

Divide the children into two groups. Line up one group at either end of the playground. Each individual child in one group should be paired with a child in the opposite group.

The game 'Chinese Whispers' demonstrates how stories can change as they are passed from one person to another.

The school grounds are ideal for creating story trails. With a ball of string children can enact the Greek myth of 'Theseus and the Labyrinth'.

A sensory walk around the school grounds introduces children to creative observation, essential for both poetry and prose.

Children's own playground games can provide a basis for the skills needed for drama.

Tackling a poetry treasure hunt is like doing a jigsaw and, as well as being fun, it helps children to look closely at the meaning of poems.

The results of children's research - perhaps into their local history - can be presented as a pageant.

Using the school grounds as their stage, children have almost unlimited scope for their drama presentations.

Language skills are practised in any survey work the children carry out.

Children use the school grounds every day for their play. Their views on the school environment can form the basis for a survey.

Tell each group to walk to the other end of the playground, in the role of someone walking a dog. Explain that, initially anyway, you want each group to ignore the other and to cross in the middle of the playground without noticing each other.

When they have done this tell them to walk back, but this time, as they cross, their dogs should begin growling at their partners' dogs. They must pull their dogs away with great difficulty. Stress, however, that all this must be suggested without any sound from anyone. This is something that can be done by everyone at once or two at a time.

Walking the dog is only one mime that can be played out walking across the playground. Here are some more suggestions:

- Wheeling a pushchair, stopping to look in a shop, looking round to find the pushchair running away.
- Carrying a load of parcels, walking into someone coming the other way.
- Carrying a ladder, meeting a friend, turning round and putting the end of the ladder through a shop window.
- Walking along reading a paper and bumping into a lamp-post.

**Parcels can obscure your view! ... 'Walking into trouble ' develops mime skills.**

Children like playing 'Walking into Trouble' but will often use it as an excuse to pull each other about. One way around this is to make a rule that no physical contact must take place. Another way is to ask the children to carry it out in slow motion.

After they have played this game, discuss how they thought they looked in their mimes. Talk about the importance of pairs working together.

## People patterns

AT1i–v

The space which is available outside also gives plenty of scope for looking at group dynamics. Talk about the job a director does in positioning actors on stage. Look at photographs and talk about the way the photographers have placed their subjects.

Now take the children outside and divide them into groups of about half a dozen. Nominate one 'photographer' in each group. Ask him or her to arrange the others for a photograph. You might like to carry out this activity for real, and actually take photographs. Children could bring in their own cameras. Alternatively you may prefer to keep it entirely in the realm of drama.

When the first child has arranged the group, nominate another to produce an entirely different picture, and so on until each child has had a turn at being the photographer. Encourage them to position children at different levels, in different postures.

When everyone has finished, you might like to give them the opportunity to arrange larger groups, perhaps the whole class.

## Street theatre

AT1i-
AT2i-

When the children have become familiar with the idea of seeing groups of people in terms of the relationships of individuals to a larger picture, ask them to set up their own street picture, made up of a series of smaller groups, like the ones they have formed for photographs.

Ask them to think about the different people they might see in the street. They could make a list of these. Then choose a suitable area to set up your street picture. There may be a long strip of land somewhere in your school grounds that has its own distinct borders, or you could just use the playground.

Ask the children to set up their groups as if they were all in the same street. Each group should tell a small story about something happening in that street. You may or may not wish to include sound, dialogue, movement or props.

Scenarios might include the following:

- A wedding group
- A protest or demonstration
- Furniture removers
- A car crash
- Road works
- Schoolchildren crossing
- Someone having a heart-attack
- A policeman dealing with a drunk
- Market stalls
- A bank robbery
- Tourists being given a guided tour

Older children could be asked to write a diary of their street. Alternatively, they might like to add detail to some of their scenarios and write them out as scripts.

**A traditional class photograph can provide a starting point for looking at people patterns.**

**As a 'photographer', each child can arrange the others in a chosen way.**

Street theatre will be enlivened by an appropriate musical accompaniment; ideas can be worked out in the classroom.

## A pageant

1i–viii

A natural development from creating group pictures of the kind described above is to hold a pageant. This can be a focus for a great deal of integrated work in Art, Science and other subjects as well as English.

A pageant is a semi-dramatic presentation of a topic. Unlike a play, which explores a situation, a pageant is usually the result of an exploration. Children who have spent a term finding out about life in Victorian England, for example, might present their findings as a series of tableaux in costume in the school grounds – a pageant of Victorian life.

These tableaux do not need to be held together by a connected sequence of events. Here we might see a scene from a workhouse such as paupers queuing for food, there a group of children playing with hoops and whipping tops, elsewhere a middle class family being waited on by servants, but none of these scenes needs to be connected by a plot or a narrative. They are interrelated in a thematic way alone.

This, of course, makes the mounting of quite a large pageant a much easier affair than a play with scenes following one after the other. Each group of children can work on the development of its own tableau independently.

Tableaux themselves can be static or dynamic. If one were to take the example of the workhouse scene given above, the children could create their own characters within the scene – they might chose to enact the story of Oliver Twist asking for more gruel, for instance – in which case, this small story would be re-enacted at regular intervals.

Pageants have the advantage of distributing the spotlight fairly evenly among the actors. They also allow children to buttress their parts with their own research. What a character lacks in the acting may be made up for in the costume or the details of the props created and these can be produced over a considerable period of time.

People tend to think of pageants in historical terms, but this need not be so. The subjects of the tableaux are limitless; they

Dragon dancing adds an element of carnival to a pageant.

might be entirely abstract, if this were desirable. So a term's work on weather, for example, could be illustrated by a series of weather tableaux in which we saw the effects of floods and winds, the processes of growth and harvesting, people in mackintoshes and others sunbathing, children holding up or weaving together threads or ribbons representing the different colours of the rainbow, and so on.

A pageant is often stationary but it can also be a processional performance. Why not add elements of carnival, like music and dancing? This can make a wonderful way of finishing off a period of research and investigation into one subject.

## A promenade performance

AT1i–viii

An alternative to moving the performers about, in the way suggested above, is to move the audience. A performance in which the action shifts from one location to another and the audience moves with the action is called a promenade.

In a promenade performance it is customary for the audience and the performers to mingle together. The audience might, for example, be watching a scene taking place in one space, when some of its members will suddenly reveal themselves to be performers by taking up the play where they stand.

It can be helpful to create a series of stages within the area of your promenade. Look for natural raised areas such as steps, on to which your performers can climb when it comes to their part of the action.

A promenade performance is often episodic. A play, for example, which told the story of two families, might take place on two stages, with the action switching from the domestic life of one family to the domestic life of the other. Scenes which involved both families might be enacted by performers from both families leaving their respective 'home' stages and moving to a third area.

A performance of this kind might also include double scenes in which the action rapidly switches between two staging areas with characters freezing when they are not speaking and then coming back to life when they return to the action.

This is very effective when the characters are commenting on each other, as in the example below. It is important, in attempting a performance of this kind, to keep the action of the play moving fluently. This means that the staging areas will need to be relatively near to each other. As one scene is ending another should be beginning elsewhere. Children will therefore need to listen very carefully to each other to know when to come in.

In many ways a play like this seems more natural to children whose own early make-believe games often involve going from place to place, creating different locations for different sets of actions.

---

# BETRAYED
## (a promenade performance)

**STAGE 1**

| | |
|---|---|
| POLICE OFFICER: | So you don't know anything about your friend Jack? |
| JILL: | I haven't got a friend called Jack. |
| POLICE OFFICER: | That's not what I've heard. |
| JILL: | Well you've heard wrong then. |
| POLICE OFFICER: | I wonder. |

*(They freeze.)*

**STAGE 2**

| | |
|---|---|
| JACK: | I suppose she'll have told them everything by now. |
| LUCY: | Of course she won't. Jill's not like that. |
| JACK: | That's what you think. |
| LUCY: | It's what I know. |

*(They freeze.)*

**STAGE 1**

| | |
|---|---|
| POLICE OFFICER: | You're making a mistake hanging around with someone like that. |
| JILL: | Someone like what? |
| POLICE OFFICER: | A thief. |
| JILL: | He's no thief. |
| POLICE OFFICER: | So you do know him? |

*(They freeze.)*

**STAGE 2**

JACK:                You wait and see. She'll give us away as soon as she opens her mouth.

LUCY:              So what are you going to do?

JACK:                I'm getting out of here.

LUCY:              Where will you go?

JACK:                I'll find a job somewhere.

LUCY:              I'm coming with you.

*(They get down off Stage 2 and begin walking towards Stage 3.)*

**STAGE 3**

MAYOR:           We need someone to deal with this giant.

COUNCILLOR:    But who can we find?

MAYOR:           Someone very brave.

COUNCILLOR:    Or very desperate.

*(They sit scratching their heads.)*

**STAGE 1**

POLICE OFFICER:  I think you'd better lead us to him.

JILL:                 What are you going to do with him?

POLICE OFFICER:  I'm afraid we'll have to arrest him.

*(They get down off Stage 1 and walk towards Stage 2. Jack and Lucy, and Jill and the police officer all go a long way round and miss each other.)*

**STAGE 2**

POLICE OFFICER:  All right, where is he, then?

JILL:                 I don't know.

POLICE OFFICER:  I haven't got time to listen to fairy stories, you know. This is a serious matter.

*(They freeze.)*

**STAGE 3**

MAYOR:           What we really need is a complete mug.

JACK:                Hello. I'm looking for a job.

COUNCILLOR:    You could be just the person we need.

## A documentary

If the school has video equipment, the children could make their own documentary about a day in the school grounds. First you will need to discuss with them what aspects of the outdoor environment should be covered: you may decide to make it a broad panorama or you may wish to concentrate on just a few features, such as playground games, the conservation area or visitors to the school.

The documentary could include interviews with pupils and members of staff; children could read their own poems about the environment; some of their games or miming activities could be recorded.

When the filming is complete, the children can edit their work and perhaps add short pieces of music where appropriate, either recorded music or their own improvised accompaniment with simple percussion instruments. The finished documentary can be presented to the whole school and perhaps to parents and other visitors.

An alternative to making a video is to put on a documentary drama on the same subject. Groups of children could act out certain events and activities that take place in the school grounds on a particular day. This could be presented as an assembly to the whole school. The children might like to look at certain issues, such as bullying in the playground.

# Language

English is the language in which all other subjects are taught, with the exception of some mother-tongue or foreign-language teaching. Consequently the work in a variety of subjects which can be carried out in the school grounds represents a vast resource for the English teacher.

There is much work that might be labelled, for example, Environmental Education because it focuses the child's observation on the external world, or Design and Technology because it is concerned with the processes of assessing a situation and drawing up a blueprint for change, all of which nevertheless involves English because the components are discussion and transactional writing.

## Mapping the school

AT1i–v

There is always a tension between the twin objectives of a school: the wish to encourage individual excellence combined with the need to produce conformity to a set of rules.

The emphasis on uniformity is expressed strongly in the design and layout of most schools. Few sites allow the development of individual rapport with the buildings and the site.

However, holding a design review of your school is a way of inviting this kind of individual engagement with the school environment. Begin by asking the children to consider what the school looks like in general. What building materials are used? What separate areas can be distinguished? How are these areas differentiated? What sort of fencing is used? Where are the paths? Are they used? Or

do pupils create their own paths? What messages does the outside of the school convey to visitors?

Ask the children to draw a plan of the school grounds. Older children could use symbols or colours to show everything that is there, including apparently minor features such as litter bins, benches and playground markings. You may also wish to ask them to provide a key to their maps.

Alternatively, or as an extension to this process, they might like to make a three-dimensional model of the grounds, using cardboard boxes, packaging and other scrap materials.

When they have completed their maps, look at them together. Discuss any aspects of the grounds that have been left out. Is there an overall message that this detailed scrutiny throws up? Does it draw attention to specific problems like graffiti, litter, shelter from weather, external seating, or signposting? What features of the school grounds attempt to solve these problems and how successful are they?

**What message does the outside of the school convey to visitors?**

## Finding out how the school grounds are used

When they have mapped the school, ask the children to investigate their own views in more detail and to find out what other users of the school think of the grounds.

One way of doing this is by carrying out a site survey. The *Esso Schoolwatch* pack, available from Learning Through Landscapes (see Resources section), provides the most effective framework for carrying this out. The pack, which contains Survey Sheets and detailed Teacher's Notes, looks at the following areas: School and Community, School Grounds, How The Grounds Are Used, and Site Management and Development.

Discuss with the children which people use the school site. The list will include pupils, teachers and support staff, as well as visitors, parents and perhaps adult learners. Can the children increase the process of consultation by getting access to the opinions of each of these groups?

### A USER QUESTIONNAIRE

One way to consult users is to send out questionnaires in the mail and you might decide that this is how you want to tackle those users who are less easy to reach, such as school governors. Another – very effective – way is to ask the children to stand in specific places in the school at certain times and to directly canvass people's opinions.

Older children can work in pairs to design their own questionnaires. Younger ones can work on a simpler version in a larger group, directed by the teacher.

First of all, they will need to decide what categories and areas of use they want to investigate. These will need to be dealt with in order. It is not desirable to produce a set of questions that dart back and forth between topics, now looking at recreation, now litter, now going back to recreation again.

They should be encouraged also to think of questions that prompt specific answers. So, for example, a question like 'What do you think of the school grounds?' is not as helpful as 'Are you happy with the number of litter

Canvassing a user's opinion of the school grounds

bins?' The questionnaires will almost certainly have to go through a drafting process before an agreed final product is reached.

The children will also need to consider whether each group of users should be faced with the same inquiries. Should parents be asked the same questions as pupils? Should questions differ for different year groups?

When the children have produced their finished questionnaires and have taken them out into the grounds to carry out the process of investigation and consultation, they will have a very large database of information. They can then go on to talk about what they have discovered and develop a series of recommendations for improvements to the grounds.

### REPORTING THE FINDINGS

AT1i–viii
AT3i–viii

Discuss with the children the shape and structure of their report. It might include, for example, quotations from the views that have been sampled, a graphical presentation of the results of the survey, or a revised site plan which takes into account the suggested improvements.

One point that is worth emphasising is that two kinds of recommendations will emerge – short-term and long-term – and they will need to be addressed to two different sets of people.

Short-term recommendations are those that can be achieved without much in the way of expense. They are effectively changes of use rather than alterations to the structure of the site. For example, when dealing with the question of litter, it might emerge that a litter bin would be more effective if its position was changed; alternatively, the children might recommend an anti-litter drive with posters designed by pupils. Similarly, on the subject of recreation, children might like to set aside an area of the grounds as a quiet reading area, or they might want to establish a ball-free zone. These are all measures which are within the control of teachers and children themselves.

The children may want to present their report, and especially these short-term recommendations, at a special assembly. This could include wall displays and three-dimensional models as well as a rehearsed talk by the children.

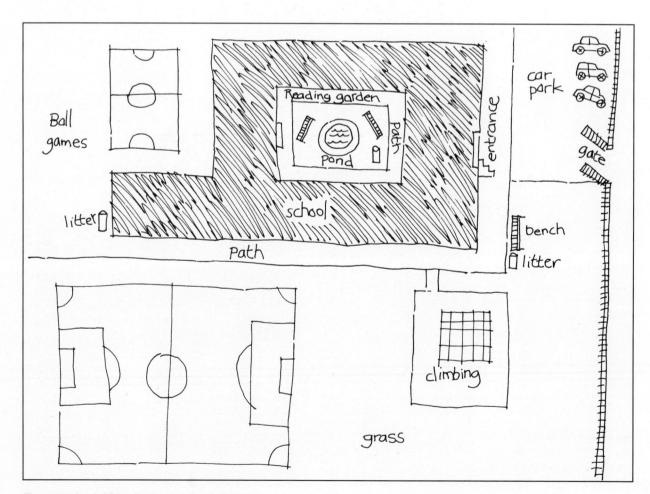

**The report might include a revised site plan.**

Long-term recommendations need to be addressed to the school governors. The children could be asked to draft a letter for the governors' consideration and send it to them with a copy of the report.

## From where I'm sitting ...

Establishing the strengths and weaknesses of your school grounds can lead to a whole series of related writing activities, particularly opportunities for descriptive writing. One way of developing children's prose description is to play 'From Where I'm Sitting ...'.

The children begin by each choosing a location in the school grounds which they are going to describe. Each child then takes a chair, sits down in his or her location and looks very carefully at the view that presents itself. Then they begin to give a detailed description of what they can see from their seats, starting with the words 'From where I'm sitting ...'. Encourage them to be as graphic and as exact as possible in their description.

Afterwards, they can write down their descriptions and read them out to the whole class who can try to find the exact spot where the writer was sitting.

'From where I'm sitting ...' – an activity that will develop children's descriptive writing abilities

AT3i–viii

## *A school guide book*

Children might be interested in producing a guide book for visitors to the school or for new pupils. As well as descriptions, it could include sections on the history of the school, school walks or trails (see page 13) as well as information about how the site is used. Pupils could illustrate it with photographs or drawings.

They might find it helpful to study a range of commercially produced advertising material, including guides and travel brochures, prospectuses for universities and colleges, hotels and holiday camps, and advertisements in newspapers and magazines.

Why not run a school pride campaign? Children could produce slogans and posters which could be put up round the school. These might have a number of objectives, such as:

- to change undesirable behaviour traits;
- to encourage friendliness;
- to discourage racism;
- to increase a sense of ownership.

Children need to decide what section of the school population they particularly want to target, what messages they want to get across and what are the most effective slogans for doing that.

**Producing a school guide book will draw on the children's observation of their environment.**

## A school newsletter

Another writing activity linked to the school environment could be the production of a newsletter. This could be produced on an occasional basis – say, once a term – and could document the seasonal changes in the school grounds, in terms of both natural features and activities taking place.

You might like to invite in a local journalist to talk to the children about writing for a newspaper. Perhaps a visit to a newspaper office could be arranged.

The production of a newsletter will provide opportunities for learning word processing skills and developing an understanding of laying out material in a way that makes it easy to read.

How can messages about the school be conveyed in an eye-catching way?

AT1
AT3

# The Playground Ghost

Poetry, like many other forms of writing, is about finding a personality and giving that personality a voice. One way of doing this is by inventing a character and looking at the world from their point of view. The effect of this is literally to see an accustomed landscape with new eyes. The playground ghost is such a character.

Talk about ghosts with the children. Ask them first whether or not they believe in ghosts. What are the reasons for their opinions? Children very often have stories to tell about ghostly happenings which they have heard from parents, friends or which they have made up themselves. Let them tell as many of these stories as they want to.

Talk about the way ghosts are said to behave. Why are they reputed to return to particular places or buildings? What do they want? What powers are they supposed to have? Are there any limits to those powers? Are ghosts invisible to everyone or can some people see them? What kind of people might these be?

Ask the children to make up a personality for their own particular ghost. Tell them to imagine that he or she haunts the school grounds. Now ask them to go out and look at the grounds as if they were the ghost. What do they see? Does it all make sense to them or not? What do they feel? Do they envy those who are alive or are they glad they don't have to go to school? Ask the children to make up a poem written by the ghost.

# The Playground Ghost

Your school grounds are haunted by a ghost. You must decide what the ghost is like. The following questions might help you.

### What is the ghost like now?

Who has seen the ghost?
Where in the grounds has the ghost been seen?
What was the ghost wearing?
Has the ghost ever spoken?

### What was the ghost like when alive?

How long ago did the ghost live?
Was your school in existence then?
If not, what was on the site?
Did the ghost live there?
Did the ghost have a family?
Did the ghost have a happy life?
Was the ghost rich or poor?
Did the ghost go to school?
How old was the ghost when he/she died?
How did the ghost die?

Now go for a walk in the school grounds. Try to imagine that you are the ghost. This is the place you are doomed to haunt.

### How does it all look to you?

What do you think of the clothes the children are wearing?
Do you recognize any of the games they are playing?
Are you surprised by any of the things you see?

### Write a poem as if you were the ghost.

# Playground Games

As any teacher knows, there is an extraordinary variety of playground rhymes and games. Talk about these with the children. Ask them to recite examples of rhymes, chants and dips. (Older children might be interested to know that one theory suggests that dipping games go back to early rituals used to find victims for human sacrifice!)

Ask them what playground games they play now and what games they played when they were younger. Pick a relatively well-known and simple game, like 'He' or 'Tag', and ask them to explain the rules.

When everyone has agreed on the rules of the game, ask the children to write them down, so that someone who had never played the game before would be able to understand it. Stress the importance of making the explanation clear and simple.

Children will find this surprisingly difficult. It might help to look first at the way rules are set out for other games, such as board games. This establishes vocabulary such as 'the

player', rather than 'you', and 'the object of the game'. It also enables them to see how instructions can be set out in a sequence of short sentences.

When they have written out the rules for the game, divide the children into groups and ask each group to chose another playground game to describe in this way. Some games which look relatively simple, such as 'Hopscotch', are very difficult indeed to describe. They may find that it helps to play the game before writing out the rules. Alternatively, this could be an opportunity for interviewing younger children about the games they play.

The children might like to create their own School Games Compendium which lists rhymes, chants and dips as well as playground games. This could be illustrated with drawings to explain games and with photographs of children playing them. They might also like to try their hand at inventing their own games for younger children.

# Playground Games

In your group, agree on the rules of a game you have played or have seen played in the school grounds. Write out the rules so that they are clear and easy to understand. You may illustrate them if you need to.

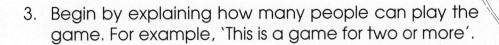

Here are a few tips to help you.

1. It is a good idea to number your instructions, like this.

2. It helps if each instruction is fairly short.

3. Begin by explaining how many people can play the game. For example, 'This is a game for two or more'.

4. If your game requires any special equipment like dice, state this.

5. If your game requires markings, a pitch, bases or posts, state this. If necessary, draw a diagram.

6. Refer to people who play the game as 'the players'. If you want to describe what different people do, call them 'the first player', 'the second player' and so on.

7. If there are different types of player, explain what they are called. For example, in the game 'He' or 'Tag' one player is called 'he'.

8. Explain what part each different type of player takes in the game.

9. Explain how the game is won, lost or otherwise comes to an end.

10. Make sure you do not leave out anything.

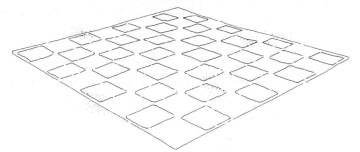

# A Weather Walk

Although direct observation of nature is taken for granted in subjects like geography and science, it is seldom seen as being necessary for English. But description depends on looking.

Read some weather poems with the children. (See the Resources section for books which contain suitable poems.) Look at details in the poems and talk about the way in which poets try to describe the effects of weather.

Talk with the children about the effects of weather on the school. How does it affect children and teachers? Do they behave differently in different kinds of weather? Why?

Take them for a walk in the grounds, or in the garden or a park, to observe its effects. Look for details: the shapes of puddles, raindrops on flowers, spiders' webs on windows, earth pock-marked by rain, icicles, children's breath coming out like steam. Look also for long-term effects of weather, such as the erosion of brick-work, the rusting of metal, or the rotting of wood. Can they find anything that has been completely destroyed by the weather?

How does the weather affect the lives of animals, such as birds and insects, worms and snails? If there is a pond in your school grounds, look at it in different weather conditions. Perhaps there are trees to observe also.

As well as looking, ask the children to use their other senses: for example, listening to the sound of the wind, feeling it on their faces.

Afterwards, tell them to imagine they are writing a letter to a friend of their own age who has been very ill and in bed for weeks. Ask them to describe what the weather is like, trying to make it seem real for their friend. Ask them to think about poets and writers they have read, and the ways in which they have used words to give a vivid impression of the weather. Now ask the children to try to do the same thing.

# A Weather Walk

Write a letter to a school friend who has been ill in bed for a long time. In your letter describe a walk you have taken in the school grounds. Talk about what the weather was like on your walk. Try to make your friend feel that he or she was there with you. Talk about how the weather made you feel, what you heard and smelled.

Here are some questions to help you.

Was it hot, warm, chilly, cold, freezing?

Did you enjoy being outside or not?

How did the weather make you feel?

Was the weather right for the time of year?

How did the school buildings and the school grounds look? Were they affected by the weather?

Were the birds, insects and other creatures affected by the weather?

What about the trees and plants, the soil, paving and tarmac?

Did the weather affect the other children in your class?

What colour was the sky?

What did the clouds look like?

Try to make your description really come alive for your friend.

# Journey of Discovery

## MAKING A MAP

Many children enjoy reading stories about animals making journeys, like the *Great Escapes* series by David Lloyd or, for older children, *Watership Down* by Richard Adams and *The Animals of Farthing Wood* by Colin Dann. Children can be encouraged to create journey stories of their own, using animal characters.

This is best done as a class together, after reading an animal journey story. First they need to decide on the main character of their stories. Then they should make their own maps of the school grounds. These should be drawn from the point of view of the animal. To such creatures a huge stretch of tarmac would not be a playground. It would be more like a desert.

Walk around the grounds with the children, looking at each different area. If a small animal was journeying through the school grounds, what path would it take? What would it make of playground markings, seats or play structures?

## PLANNING THE JOURNEY

Now ask the children to decide why the animal makes the journey. Is it looking for food or a new home? Does it have any companions? What happens to the animal on the journey? Does it meet any enemies, human or otherwise? Does it get lost? Perhaps it cannot finish the journey in one night and has to hide in the grounds during the day.

## TELLING THE STORY

The children might like to tell the story in the first person, imagining they were telling other animals what happened to them.

# Journey of Discovery

You are going to make up a story about a journey made by an animal through your school grounds.

Use this worksheet to help you plan the journey.

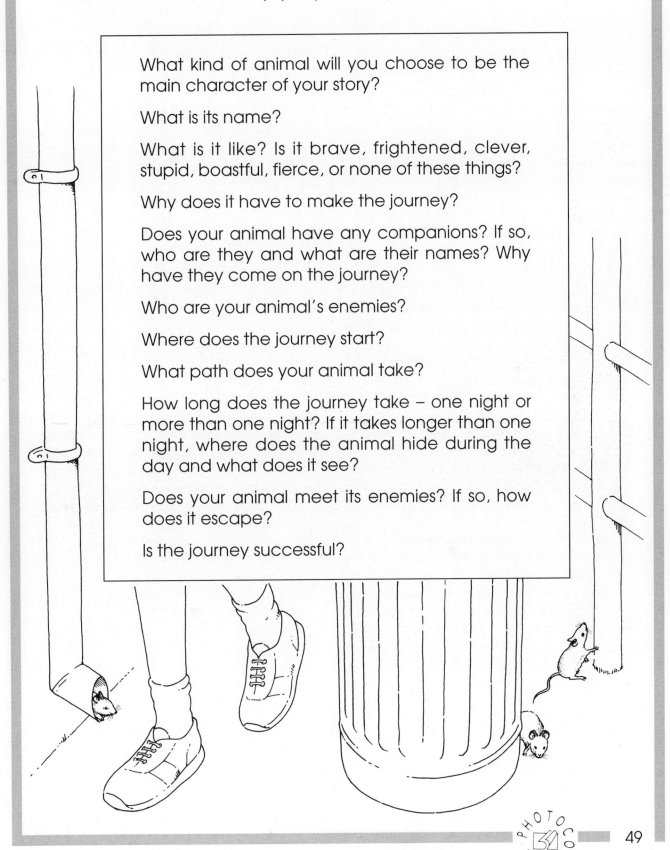

What kind of animal will you choose to be the main character of your story?

What is its name?

What is it like? Is it brave, frightened, clever, stupid, boastful, fierce, or none of these things?

Why does it have to make the journey?

Does your animal have any companions? If so, who are they and what are their names? Why have they come on the journey?

Who are your animal's enemies?

Where does the journey start?

What path does your animal take?

How long does the journey take – one night or more than one night? If it takes longer than one night, where does the animal hide during the day and what does it see?

Does your animal meet its enemies? If so, how does it escape?

Is the journey successful?

# Safety in the School Grounds

Finding out and processing information is a skill that is required by subjects right across the curriculum. Learning how to ask questions and interpret the answers so as to provide useful information is therefore a valuable skill. One area that can be beneficial for children to investigate is personal safety.

Begin by talking to them about what they do in the school grounds. What is meant by the word 'play'? Are there other things that go on that would not be called 'play'? Do the children encounter any problems in the school grounds? Do accidents ever happen?

Ask them about children in other year groups. Are the grounds used differently by older and younger children? Do children from different year groups mix in the grounds?

When the children have talked about their own views, explain that to get a complete picture they need to find out the views of other people who use the school grounds. They will almost certainly need to talk to playground helpers, who keep a record of accidents in the playground. You could invite one of the helpers into the class to talk to the children.

The children will need to think about what information they want to find out. Then they should decide how to ask the questions so

that people can give a simple YES/NO answer.

Older children can work in pairs. Each pair could deal with a different aspect of safety in the school grounds. These could include: accidents involving balls, skipping ropes or other play equipment; accidents caused by children running into each other; bullying and fighting; cuts caused by glass or other sharp objects. Younger children may need to work in a larger group, directed by the teacher.

As well as finding out about things that have happened, they might also enquire into what people think of measures that could be adopted to improve safety. Such measures might include creating separate areas for ball games, including more seats, making different areas for different year groups.

When each pair (or group) has thought up a series of questions, the teacher could write them all out on the board (or photocopy them) so that each pair can use the complete list of questions to carry out their interviews.

The children should conduct their research in the school grounds, interviewing as many people as possible. Afterwards the results can be written up as part of a School Safety Manual.

# Safety in the School Grounds

You are going to make a questionnaire to find out whether people think the school grounds are safe.

Use this worksheet to help you design your questionnaire.

## What dangers are you going to find out about?

What dangers can you think of in your school grounds?
What sort of accidents happen?
Make a list of them and decide which ones to investigate.

## Who are you going to ask?

To find out what dangerous things happen, you will need to ask other pupils. Do you need to ask anyone else?

## How are you going to put the questions?

You need to ask questions that have simple answers, preferably YES or NO. For example, you might ask, 'Have you ever been hit by a ball?' But it is no good going on to ask 'How did it happen?' That is too vague. 'Where did it happen?' is clearer. It would be even clearer to ask:

Did it happen:  (a) in the playground?
                (b) in the grassed area?
                (c) in the car park?

This is just an example from a school with three separate areas in its grounds. Your school grounds may be different.

## What will you do with the results of your questionnaire?

The answers to your questions will tell you what people think of the school grounds. This will give you ideas for making the grounds safer. Discuss your ideas with your teacher.

# Resources

## USEFUL ORGANIZATIONS

All of these organizations produce a range of resources that will help in developing ideas in this book.

Common Ground
c/o London Ecology Centre
45 Sheldon Street
London WC2 9HJ

English & Media Centre
Sutherland Street
London SW1

Friends of the Earth
26-28 Underwood Street
London N1 7JQ

Learning through Landscapes
Third Floor, Southside Offices
The Law Courts
Winchester
Hants SO23 9DL

Living Archive
Stantonbury Campus
Stantonbury
Milton Keynes
Bucks. MK14 6BN

National Association for Environmental
    Education
Wolverhampton Polytechnic
Walsall Campus
Gorway
Walsall
West Midlands WS1 3BD

National Association for Urban Studies
Lewis Cohen Urban Studies Centre
University of Brighton
68 Grand Parade
Brighton BN2 2JY

National Children's Play and Recreation Unit
359-361 Euston Road
London NW1 3AL

Royal Society for the Protection of Birds
The Lodge
Sandy
Beds. SG19 2DL

Tidy Britain Group
The Pier
Wigan WN3 4EX

WATCH/Royal Society for Nature
    Conservation
The Green
Witham Park
Waterside South
Lincoln LN5 7JR

World Wide Fund for Nature
Panda House
Weyside Park
Catteshall Lane
Godalming
Surrey GU7 1XR

# BIBLIOGRAPHY

## Poetry

Books for teaching poetry:

*On Common Ground*, Jill Pirrie (WWF, 1987)
*Catching The Light*, Brian Moses (WWF, 1991)
*The Green Umbrella*, Jill Brand with Wendy Blows and Caroline Short (WWF, 1991)
*The Oxford Dictionary of Nursery Rhymes*, Iona and Peter Opie (Oxford University Press, 1951)

Good anthologies of poems for reading outside:

*The Four Seasons* series (*Spring, Summer, Autumn, Winter*), Jennifer Wilson (Simon & Schuster Young Books, 1989)
*A Year Full of Poems*, Michael Harrison and Christopher Stuart-Clark (Oxford University Press, 1991)
*Occasions*, Anne Harvey (Blackie, 1990)
*Let's Celebrate: Festival Poems*, John Foster (Oxford University Press, 1989)
*What On Earth*, Judith Nicholls (Faber & Faber, 1989)

## Story

*Limited Damage*, Brian Keaney (Learning through Landscapes, 1991)
*School Under Siege* (English & Media Centre)

Books referred to in story activities:

*Moondial*, Helen Cresswell (Faber & Faber)
*Watership Down*, Richard Adams (Penguin, 1974)
*The Animals of Farthing Wood*, Colin Dann (Heinemann, 1979)
*Jack the Dog, Mot the Mouse, Lady Loudly the Goose, Tumult the Rabbit, Waldo the Tortoise, Romeo and Juliet the Lovebirds*, David Lloyd (Walker)
*The Very Hungry Caterpillar*, Erich Carle (Hamish Hamilton, 1986)
*The Very Cross Ladybird*, Erich Carle (Hamish Hamilton, 1986)

The following books are aimed at older children but may still be useful:

*Making Stories*, Bronwyn Mellor, Mike Raleigh, Paul Ashton (English & Media Centre, 1984)
*Changing Stories*, Bronwyn Mellor, Judith Hemming, Jane Leggett (English & Media Centre, 1984)
*Reading Stories*, Bronwyn Mellor (English & Media Centre, 1988)

## Drama

Useful books for creating your own ceremonies and celebrations:

*The Months Of The Year*, Paul Hughes (Young Library, 1982)
*The Customs and Ceremonies of Britain*, Charles Kightly (Thames & Hudson, 1986)

## Language

*Esso Schoolwatch* pack (Learning through Landscapes, 1992)
*Green Ink*, Elizabeth Allen (WWF, 1990)
*Eco School*, Pru Poulton and Gillian Symons (WWF, 1990)

# National Curriculum Attainment Targets and Programmes of Study

This book provides activities for all three Profile Components of the National Curriculum for English:

Speaking and Listening
Reading
Writing

## Attainment Targets

The activities suggested in this book meet many of the Attainment Targets in the National Curriculum for English at Key Stages 1, 2 and 3 (Levels 1 to 8).

**SPEAKING AND LISTENING** tasks are integrated throughout the book. In particular in the section on Drama, children are required to:

Participate as speakers and listeners in group activities, including imaginative play (Level 1).

Respond appropriately to simple instructions given by a teacher (Level 1).

Participate as speakers and listeners in a group engaged in a given task (Level 2).

Relate real or imaginary events in a connected narrative which conveys meaning to a group of pupils, the teacher or another known adult (Level 3).

Participate in a presentation, e.g. of the outcome of a group activity, a poem, a story, a scene (Level 4).

Plan and participate in a presentation, e.g. of the outcome of a group activity, a poem, a story, a scene (Level 5).

Participate in simple presentations or performances with some fluency (Level 6).

Talk about the contribution that facial expressions, gestures and tone of voice can make to a speaker's meaning (Level 8).

**READING** tasks also occur throughout the book, but are most commonly found in the sections on Poetry and Story where children are required to:

Talk in simple terms about the content of stories (Level 1).

Listen and respond to stories, poems and other material read aloud, expressing opinions informed by what has been read (Level 2).

Listen attentively to stories, talk about setting, story line and characters and recall significant details (Level 3).

Read aloud expressively, and with fluency, from a range of familiar literature (Level 4).

Read a range of fiction and poetry, explaining their preferences in talk and writing (Level 5).

Read a range of fiction and poetry, including works not written specifically for children, explaining their preferences in talk and writing (Level 6).

Talk about some of the effects of sound patterning (Level 7).

Talk and write about their responses to literature, taking account of matters such as dramatic, poetic or fictional structure, complexities of plot, development of character and theme and the use of poetic or stylistic devices (Level 8).

**WRITING** tasks can also be found throughout the book. In the sections on Story and Language in particular, children are required to:

Use pictures, symbols or isolated letters, words or phrases to communicate meaning (Level 1).

Write stories showing an understanding of the

rudiments of story structure, establishing an opening, characters and one or more events (Level 2).

Write more complex stories with detail beyond simple events and with a defined ending (Level 3).

Write stories which have an opening, a setting, characters, a series of events, and a resolution; produce other kinds of chronologically organized writing such as instructions and accounts (Level 4).

Write in a variety of forms, e.g. notes, letters, instructions, stories, poems, for a range of purposes, e.g. to plan, to inform, to express attitudes or emotions (Level 5).

Write in a variety of forms for a range of purposes, showing some ability to present subject matter differently for different specified known audiences (Level 6).

Write in a wider variety of forms, for a wider range of purposes (Level 7).

Write in a wide variety of forms with a more assured sense of purpose, organizing and presenting subject matter appropriately for specified audiences both known and unknown. Produce a sustained piece of writing when the task demands it (Level 8).

## Programmes of Study

The activities suggested in this book fulfil many of the general and detailed provisions of the Programmes of Study for all three Profile Components at Key Stages 1, 2 and 3. These are generally recursive and include:

### Reading
Activities should ensure that pupils:

Hear books, stories and poems read aloud and take part in shared reading experiments with other pupils and the teacher, using texts composed and dictated by the pupils themselves, as well as rhymes, poems, songs and familiar stories (including traditional stories from a variety of cultures).

Read in the context of role-play and dramatic play.

Re-tell, re-read or dramatise familiar stories and poems.

Have opportunities to participate in all activities related to reading, e.g. preparing and reading a selection of poems, or reciting some from memory, or taking part in storytelling sessions or dramatic activities.

Read aloud to the class or teacher.

### Writing
Activities should ensure that pupils:

Undertake a range of chronological writing including some at least of diaries, stories, letters, accounts of tasks they have done and of personal experience, records of observations they have made.

Undertake a range of non-chronological writing which includes some at least of lists, captions, labels, invitations, greetings cards, notices, posters, plans and diagrams, descriptions, e.g. of a person or place, and notes for an activity.

Write individually and in groups, sharing their writing with others and discussing what they have written.

Write in response to a range of well-chosen stories, poems or plays.

Have frequent opportunities to write in different contexts and in a wide range of activities.

Recognize that writing involves decision making, when the context is established.

### Speaking and Listening
Activities should ensure that pupils:

Encounter a range of situations and activities which are designed to develop their competence, precision and confidence in speaking and listening, including working with other pupils and adults.

Listen and respond to stories, rhymes, poems

and songs, familiar and unfamiliar. These should include examples from pupils' own work.

Plan collaborative activities.

Tell stories and recite poems which have been learnt by heart.

Work with or devise drama scripts.

Use and understand the use of role-play.

In the course of group activity, engage constructively in prediction, speculation and hypothesis.